TERSE VERSE
A Collection of Poetry
BY: C. TOM HOWES

Copyright 2020 by C. Tom Howes

All rights reserved, including the right of reproduction in whole or in part in any form.

Library of Congress Control Number: 2020942573

ISBN 978-1-932109-55-9

Cover by Chloe Fisher

Printed in the United States of America

Ross & Perry Publishing

Acknowledgements

I'd like to thank Dr.George Ross Fisher III, and The Right Angle Club, for it was there that George and I first discussed the terse verses and the suggestion for the book was given.

Introduction to Terse Verse

Haiku is brief, so let's be Brief.

We live in an ocean of words and information that demands our attention and often threatens to drown us. To combat this we must sort out the news and knowledge to determine what is important and what should be discarded.

One way of fighting this onslaught is to be more selective in what we hear and what we read. It is difficult if not impossible to read every word or every article in a newspaper. Instead, we usually scan the headlines and then choose. In business, executives pick the summaries and skip over the details. In reading a book, the plot is better remembered, as the characters and descriptions fade into the background. With Haiku, it's so brief, you often must read it twice to "get" it.

In literature, poetry presents ideas in a more compact form, fitting the thoughts in an appropriate format. Sometimes those thoughts can appear complex like a code that must be cracked. Other times the poem is much more simple and is more quickly understood. Rhymed or unrhymed, whether Haiku, sonnet, or blank verse, poems must be able to establish a connection between the writer and the reader to communicate ideas.

In *Terse Verse* the format boils down to presenting ideas and observation on human behavior and American culture using idioms, puns, and wordplay that can be easily read and enjoyed. The key to effectiveness is simplicity and the key to simplicity is brevity. And that is what *Terse Verse* is about in a nutshell.

Home Plate

Child hood
Tastes good
Mom cooked
Dad looked
Each meal
Stays real
Stays part
Ones heart

When wed
Food fed
His growl
Claims foul
Hew threat
Safe bet
Ends shout
Eat out

Fork Lift

Watch guest
Taste test
Sits up
Right cup
No slurp
Nor burp
Each bite
Chews right

Best poise
Sweet noise
Nice wife
Trim knife
Show class
Not brass
Makes tune
Gold spoon

Spice Aisles

Foods taste
Like paste
Each lunch
Lacks punch
Tongue needs
Fresh feeds
Seeks bite
With might

Cruise stores
Read lores
In quest
For zest
Smell Vials
Thyme trials
Wise age
Chews sage

Beef Stakes

Bulls goad
Rage road
Chomp chops
Risk tops
Poor guess
Eat less
Rich time
Feast prime

Most bow
Cow tow
Not stirred
Join herd
Sweet kind
Stay grind
Their deal
Kid's meal

Boar Wars

Fork fulls
Pork pulls
Lures taste
Pads waist
Mind knows
Means woes
But urge
Scores surge

Comes night
Dawns plight
Toss turn
Guts churn
Hog meals
Bring squeals
Food bouts
Pig outs

Beer Bust

Way back
Six pack
Was what
You got
Work outs
Stopped stouts
Till gyms
Just whims

Then flow
Brought woe
Shape shout
Goes out
Waist slumps
Bum bumps
Guts norm
Keg form

Burn Outs

Big meals	When food
Best deals	Fast chewed
Mouth feasts	It fires
Like beasts	Hot wires
Then night	Old spice
Brings plight	Strikes twice
Spreads snacks	Past spree
Charge back	Eats me

Haste Waist

Drive thrus	Gulps fries
Fast Chews	King size
Can't wait	Belt swells
Serve Plate	Gut jells
Those bits	Square meals
Not lites	Old deals
Grab eats	New pounds
Quick treats	Make rounds

Up Tight

Juice cap
Won't snap
Twist turn
Squeeze Churn
Non stop
No pop
Stays stuck
Curse luck

Bang nudge
Can't budge
Pound cut
Still shut
Hands wreck
Pain neck
It's glued
Both screwed

Juice Up

From fail
To hail
None stay
Same way
Can lose
Choose booze
Or stop
Go top

Each burn
You learn
Turn muff
To tough
Sad shapes
Sour grapes
Bright shine
Find wine

Pots Luck

Most fasts
Soon lasts
Vows made
Soon fade
Know thin
Won't win
Spouse half
Gets laugh

Friends joke
Bulge poke
Guts churn
Stem stern
Tho try
Same I
Belts whine
Bot line

Brews Haws

Drink up
Drain cup
Once down
Pops clown
Arm bends
Make friends
Ends foam
Head home

Comes dawn
Laughs gone
Toe stirs
Eye blurs
Look me
Tips see
Gone stout
Tapped out

Smoke Rings

Signs Sneer
Not here
Off sites
No lights
They fume
Spurn doom
Sneak scoff
Choose cough

Groups meet
Rain sleet
Friends shout
Butts out
Try quit
That's it
But hacks
Pick packs

Ah Mes

Some thrill
When ill
Itch ache
Sprain break
From vague
To plague
Love whine
Sick line

That wail
Won't fail
Docs care
Oaths swear
Hear moan
Treat groan
Rich yield
Well healed

Wind Down

Youth scene	When grown
Smoke screen	Change tone
Buy fags	Cure ills
Struts brags	Patch pills
Hot stuff	Now know
Huff puff	Real woe
Wise crack	Use wits
Then hack	Call quits

Bed Bugs

Germs crawl	Old days
Colds call	Mom's ways
Those poor	Soup rest
Quick cure	Were best
Check ads	Help keep
Drug fads	Costs cheap
Trust pills	Toll bell
Treat ills	All's well

Cure All

Sick days	Up side
Time weighs	As bide
When docs	That pain
Shun clocks	May wane
Must sit	Fade ills
Teeth grit	No bills
Wait stew	Sounds bell
Aches brew	Alls well

Shrink Raps

Psych songs	Squirms pose
Sing wrongs	Highs lows
First line	Fears sins
I'm fine	Vain spine
Change pitch	Hope spiel
Then switch	Helps heal
Play ball	Rite beat
Tell all	Rap sheet

Knock Offs

Back street
Deals neat
Styles grand
Names brand
Sales great
Sham bait
Quick look
Takes hook

Crowds dash
Plunk cash
Trash sold
Faux gold
Con's need
Fool's greed
Rich cat?
Copy that

Bald Head

Head games
Have names
Tops thin
Show skin
Turn gray
Which style
Earns smile

One group
Opts toup
May try
Do dye
Locks dread
Shave head
Choice there
Hide hair

Old Hates

Men's wear
Lacks flair
Wives jeer
Head gear
Top toe
Looks woe
Can't wait
Up date

Urge buys
Clothes ties
Ditch torn
Toss worn
Rags out
New tout
Have style
Go viral

Yo Yo

Wake up
Shake up
Toe down
Go down
Tush up
Push up
Bear down
Wear down

Up light
Up tight
Down eats
Down sweets
Up pounds
Up rounds
Down lasts
Down casts

Tote All

Springs falls
Shop malls
Sales swarm
Lines form
Wives buy
Guys sigh
She calls
He hauls

In sum
Men numb
While mate
Fills plate
As store
Sells more
Thinks large
Takes charge

Rough Shod

Males shop
Quick stop
Fast views
Buy shoes
Just one
Then done
No shout
In out

Wife's style
Can rile
Long treks
Hunts pecks
Heals toes
Arch foes
Feet stride
Fits tied

Churn Pike

Cars crawl
Swerve stall
Lines stop
Then pop
Curse cry
Fists fly
Hearts race
Slow pace

Blue sights
Red lights
All blame
Rush game
Near crash
Teeth gnash
Jaws block
Grit Lock

Red I

Take flight
Late night
Then reap
Less sleep
Dull drone
Aches bone
Comes morn
Nerves worn

Next day
You pay
Feel blue
Gray through
Last stop
Eyes pop
Face sags
Claims bags

Clothes Hoarse

Malls shout
Buy out
Go spree
Spend free
Sale thrills
Ring tills
Love yak
Haul stack

Back bends
Call friends
More squeels
Boast deals
Shout wins
Voice thins
End stress
Speech less

Hair Looms

Where skin
Meets thin
Then guys
Seek guise
Must save
Each wave
In vain
Save mane

First loops
Next toupes
Wear mops
On tops
Yet neat
Heaps heat
Locks swarm
Wig warm

Head Lines

Some hair
Stays there
From brim
To trim
Time's plow
Shapes brow
As dome
Nears chrome

Male plan
Mane man
Seek highs
Plugs dyes
Hope sprouts
Stand out
Till grays
Part ways

Foot Race

Wife sails
Boot sales
Sneaks spikes
Pump likes
Comb styles
Slow miles
Drifts spends
Cruise ends

He'll shop
One stop
His shtick
Quick pick
Then wait
Till mate
Claims win
Shoe in

Red Rug

Stars glow
Big show
Make scene
Get seen
Flout fames
Drop names
Count down
Best gown

Right dress
Wows press
If slip
Tears rip
Streaks spew
Words blue
Blush dread
Code red

Tread Mill

Buy books
For looks
They go
For show
Some day
I may
Do deed
Sit read

Chores too
Let brew
Done not
Run hot
End race
Same place
Self beat
Dead heat

Wry Breds

Matched wits	Those prim
Good fits	Act grim
When find	This fringe
Like kind	Oft cringe
Quick share	Smile zipped
Laughs fair	Tight lipped
Fun kin	Their taste
Shoe in	Straight laced

Marked Man

Proud schools	If try
Tout rules	Eeek by
Hope youth	Ad lib
Learns truth	Plea crib
Grind way	Live free
Grade A	Earns C
First prize	Their ilk
Creams rise	Sour milk

Size Up

Shop trip
Once hip
Each aisle
Now trail
Hear clothes
Shout nos
Styles quit
Fail fit

For years
No fears
Just try
Quick buy
New gains
Bring pains
Stretch pants
Fat's chance

Gilt Trip

Gem sale
Rings wail
Gals much
Love touch
Eyes squint
Stars glint
Their prayers
To wear

Buy word
Is heard
First oohs
Then choose
She's bold
Digs gold
From mine
To mine

Cast Offs

Here's tips
Cruise ships
Watch cash
Hide stash
Fun rules
Shun fools
Swim dive
High five

Shop wise
Nice buys
Knick knack
Brought back
oft junk
Thrills sunk
Sad fix
Deep six

Knit Pick

Watch threads
Weave heads
Make wig
Hairs big
Brow hid
By grid
High strung
New young

Friends guess
Tease tress
They smile
Brash style
Looks cool
Not fool
Smile long
Head strong

Depth Charged

Hit trails
Haunt sales
Greed voice
Makes choice
Friends urge
Buy splurge
Be free
Go spree

Then bills
Bring chills
Now path
New math
Rules win
Cash in
Gone tout
Charge out

Hole Truth

Golf woes
Highs lows
Bad clubs
Cause flubs
Iron curves
Rough nerves
When done
Still fun

Round ends
Join friends
Time for
Real score
Let's all
Have ball
Now we
Par tee

High Lights

My gray
Can't stay
Hear pride
Say hide
Hold still
Young thrill
Hair snow
Must go

First pause
Root cause
Right touch
Does much
Best shade
Won't fade
Top score
Dye for

Gold Bugs

Gals nag
Seek swag
Haw hems
Wish gems
Use wiles
Heap piles
Men curse
Guard purse

Sly digs
Strike bigs
Can bring
New bling
Dredge guilt
Reap gilt
Hope pout
Pans out

Head Ways

High hats	Hip track
Wear spats	Laid back
Wall Street	Ball caps
Ties neat	Fist slaps
Big bucks	Shag tops
Black tux	Flip flops
Clothes spiff	Trend now
Hair stiff	Low brow

Mend Ways

Youth's mode	Old brave
Dress code	Try save
If torn	Take care
Not worn	Each tear
Used clothes	Take yarn
Out goes	Give darn
This haste	Save dough
Makes waste	So sew

Fowl Fare

Eggs break
Boil bake
Hens die
Then fry
Their clan
Feeds man
Chick crew
Will do

Cows steers
Give cheers
In brief
Skip beef
Their feat
No meat
Plate full
No bull

Dog Gone

Watch pets
On nets
They gaffe
You laugh
Once eye
Pick buy
Hearts win
Soon kin

Love talk
Feed walk
Smiles tears
Good years
Sad days
Heart stays
Old bows
Still wows

Boot Camp

Shoe piles
All styles
Need pair
To wear
When done
Have one
Hunt wait
Find mate

Can't catch
Make match
Odd fly
Reach sky
Stray far
Near star
Black holes
Lost soles

Foot Age

Gals thurst
Feet first
Hate wear
One pair
New styles
Spout smiles
Keep score
Need more

From straps
To snaps
Have fits
Walks sits
Fast paced
Straight laced
Lips speak
Tongue chic

Clothes Call

No form
Is norm
Same styles
Cause riles
Most stay
Old way
New itch
Wild pitch

Leave home
On own
World vast
Try blast
Best fit
Scores hit
Yes man
Grand slam

Bumps Grinds

Work days
Pains praise
Jobs tough
Tasks rough
Crews brave
Sweat slave
Feels traps
Bad raps

Bless few
Tried true
Scoff scars
Bear jars
Right chops
Reach tops
If bland
Get canned

Prides Head

Take care
Lush hair
Cut shape
Nip nape
Keep trim
Roar vim
Looks snare
Lion's share

Bald face
Worst case
Stop stress
Save stress
Your thing
Rule king
Game plan
Mane man

Odds Job

Lights blaze
Minds glaze
Hope looms
Glitzed rooms
Cons wait
Slots bait
Dream eyes
High rise

Wheel turns
Purse burns
Net worth
Down earth
Home stretch
Last catch
Lucks choke
Flat broke

Take Outs

Clocks chime
Meal time
She cooks
He looks
When tires
Same fires
Wants change
Home range

Gets wish
Served dish
Best scene
They clean
At end
Must spend
Done sup
Fork up

Fling Time

Wind fall
Run mall
Cash flush
Feel rush
Strut store
Spend more
Buy on
Near gone

Heart skips
Blue chips
New lot
White hot
Splurge scene
Floods green
Big dread
Code red

Light Weights

Praise smart	When buff
Tongue tart	Just bluff
Their wit	Those shouts
Score hit	Burn outs
Loud voice	Man more
Earns choice	Than roar
Bright spars	Real bites
Poke stars	Win fights

Mark's Word

Meek born	Old game
Tin Horn	Stays same
Think lode	You bet
Down road	They get
Seek Switch	Still try
With rich	Hands high
Cons wait	Hopes sunk
Fix fate	Say "Unc"

Smart Wons

Quiz days
Eyes daze
Dim find
Slow mind
Much stress
Must guess
Low scale
Then fail

Nerds pass
Show class
Cram strain
Stretch brain
Win chase
First place
Edge foes
By knows

Cats Fat

By some
Called bum
Sleeps play
All day
"Neath skin
Soon kin
Says blog
Top dog

If itch
Strike rich
Odds long
Bet strong
Right pick
Lott tick
Life soft
Scratch oft

Bird Brains

Folks stash
Goods cash
Banks cave
Try save
Hope stay
Rain day
First leg
Nest egg

Bold step
Trust rep
Stock fling
Takes wing
Right buy
Fly high
Bad luck
Dead duck

Jets Set

Planes still
Bring thrill
Wild zooms
Big booms
Fans hail
Clouds trail
Get go
Free show

Hear roars
Blood pours
Winged slate
Worth wait
Fast flight
Grand site
Scan skies
Soar eyes

Bar Code

Ends day	Beer busts
Starts play	Prime lusts
Friends meet	When wed
Drink treat	Have fled
Old pals	Creeps flit
New gals	Hope hit
Rules done	Pitch falls
Have fun	Pub crawls

Squares Wan

Now Crowd	Gray group
Whoops loud	Out loop
Lights flash	Shapes sag
Curves brash	Wheels drag
Stay wired	Had turn
'Ner tired	Slow churn
Ring sounds	Spin done
Make rounds	Home spun

Eye Cues

Guys wise
Watch eyes
From blink
To wink
Each view
Gives clue
Quick glance
Means chance

Good looks
Great hooks
High brows
Win wows
Whip lash
Adds dash
Wed views
Eye dos

Road Ways

High way
Nerves fray
Lights stops
Kooks cops
Speed traps
Miss haps
No strain
Choose train

Take track
Out back
Just me
Stress free
End rounds
Safe sound
No mess
Wreak less

Road Hogs

Pigs fly
Zoom by
Switch lanes
Speed pains
Cars curse
Think worse
Wild swerves
Race nerves

Most fear
Crash near
Cop chase
Ends race
Hear swine
Beg whine
Trail ends
Jail pens

Queen Be

Her quest
Bee best
Must try
Score high
Spout facts
Write tracts
Buzz zeal
Sweet deal

Choice made
Cards played
Fast track
Earns jack
Right pick
Wins trick
Last sting
Trumps king

Time Lapse

Stand speak
Words freak
Brain freeze
Lips seize
Mind blanks
Tongue tanks
Just pray
What say

Try laugh
At gaff
But crowd
Moans loud
Fake cool
Look fool
No friends
Wits ends

Face Off

When gone
Swan song
Who writes
Claims rights
Picks facts
Spin acts
Slap dash
Grubs cash

They paint
Truth faint
Tout stains
Sale gains
Their views
Part trues
Friends see
Taint me

Heads Up

Look down
Coin found
This clue
Hooks you
Means luck
Has struck
Real wish
Catch fish

So kneel
Quick feel
Prize looms
Face blooms
Hopes high
Then sigh
Why glum?
Dad hum

Chop Shop

Set sail
For sale
Where crowd
Mills loud
Long lines
Test spines
Shout stores
"Spend more"

Vast sea
Park free
All barge
To charge
Bump buy
That's why
They call
It maul

Biz Buzz

Men meet
Chat greet
Eyes lock
Fists knock
Then food
Sets mood
Talk shop
Non stop

These meals
Do deals
Words hum
Near numb
Drone on
Wax strong
Wins see
King bee

Lug Age

Air port
Time short
Long wait
At age
Check signs
Tag lines
Stay near
Check gear

Crowds packed
Seats stacked
Totes squeezed
None pleased
Jet lags
Lose bags
Rushed trip
Lost grip

More Less

Old plea	First track
New me	Scale back
Hearts vow	Shed pounds
Start now	Square rounds
Use force	To lose
Change course	Heads choose
Takes guts	For win
Bust butts	Tails spin

Gag Rule

Words mean	Heads hot
Cause scene	On spot
Those near	Wise wait
Feel fear	Teeth grate
Tip toe	Shun fool
Talk show	Laws cool
Bite tongue	Chokes hold
None stung	Case cold

Rip Tied

Birth day
Kids play
Gifts zoom
Flood rooms
Friends throng
Sing song
Noise zings
Cake springs

Hands flare
Claw tear
Dive in
Shread grin
Bows heap
Trash deep
All clap
Give wrap

"Dow"n Beat

Prize seat
Wall Street
Watch wheels
Spin deals
Bears bulls
Push pulls
News rocks
Bonds stocks

Tune starts
Check charts
Buy sell
Till bell
Note gong
Ends song
Floor roars
Counts scores

All's Fair

Scribes go
New show
Write raves
Make waves
Must see
Ads plea
Fans flock
Round block

Crowds view
Then stew
Hopes dash
Was trash
They boo
Bo Bo
Twas so
So so

Why Knot

Bad days
Cause craze
Fists clench
Guts wrench
Cheeks burn
Then turn
Head spin
Can't win

Mind pleas
"At ease"
Let loose
Life's noose
Take care
If snare
When rough
Hang tough

Spare Change

Two tales
Of wails
Tire pops
Car stops
Check trunk
Just junk
Sad plea
Why me?

Next case
Poor place
Begs shout
Hand out
Dig deep
End cheap
Both folk
Flat broke

Joke Hold

Laughs please
Shticks please
Truth hides
'Neath snides
Quick fun
Sly pun
Crowds roar
Beg more

Stars host
Rib roast
Wits feast
Fools fleeced
When dine
Punch Line
Gaffs snag
Last gag

Pets Rock

Dogs heed
Your lead
Pups hound
Love found
Fast fond
Swift bond
Young old
Love hold

Kits cute
Tricks hoot
Cats muse
Pick choose
Play cool
Now rule
Furs shine
Purr lion

Fee Lines

That pet
You get
Once waif
Now safe
Swift lure
Sweet purr
Loves awe
Soft paw

Start ditch
Rags rich
They rule
Act cool
Best perk
Don't work
Prize catch
From scratch

Field Day

Pols told
Find gold
Tax trend
Must spend
Plow deep
Then reap
Friend's shout
Bale out

Who pays
Those ways
All know
Who'll owe
Rich stay
Hay day
Poor draw
Short straw

Wit Lash

Gad flies
Cause cries
Won't mind
Cross line
Stir pots
Love hots
They nag
Then brag

No rest
From jest
Nips zings
Buzz stings
Keep foes
On toes
Dogs wail
Wag's tale

Peek Boo

Lose keys
Drop knees
Not there
But where
Feel wimp
Like simp
Hear taunts
Search haunts

Steps stairs
Seek lairs
Curse plea
Oyl see
End plight
Plain sight
Blind side
Pop eyed

Dream Job

Gals yen
Bad men
Set hooks
Great looks
Abs arms
Ooze charms
Her need
Proud steed

Checks field
Poor yield
Best ones
Long wons
Rest guys
No prize
What's there?
Knight mare

Split Ends

Friends dine
Food wine
Share meals
Talk deals
Comes bill
Their drill
Smile laugh
Pay half

Turns out
Those stout
Oft choose
Prime booze
Now wise
Check size
Stop touch
Go Dutch

Crass Act

Year book
Gives look
Shows cast
Of past
Splash notes
Faux quotes
Word games
Slang names

Kind phrase
Brings praise
Smart style
Sprouts smile
Friends dear
Hearts cheer
Class Clowns
Brass sounds

Scram Bull

Mad cow
Like Dow
Oft still
Moves thrill
Quick change
Stock range
Risk makes
High steaks

Bears wait
Buck bait
Boom words
Charge herds
Each side
Tests tide
All fear
Bum steer

Foot Bawl

Crowds scream
"Go team"
Feet move
Seek groove
Play starts
Stout hearts
Cheer tricks
Get kicks

Points score
Fans roar
Cleats track
Make sack
Win game
Earn fame
Not champ
Boot camp

Off Hook

Poor fish
Soon dish
If caught
Life naught
Once free
Roamed sea
Choice grim
Sink swim

One cure
Shun lure
Shut mouth
Swim south
If wait
Take bait
Lose brains
Net gains

Knock Out

Words might
Rile fight
Up front
Boast grunt
Act bold
Won't fold
Rules rare
Fouls fair

Use wits
Duck hits
Well manned
You stand
Win day
O K
No go
K O

Shell Shock

Birth day
Fowl play
Can't roam
Egg home
First fight
Scratch bite
Break neck
Hunt peck

With luck
Can duck
Lack will
Lay still
Join group
In coop
Crack fool
Roost rule

Fly Ways

Eggs hatch
Start scratch
Next test
Leave nest
Crane neck
Hunt peck
Hens need
Chick feed

Food chains
Bird brains
Last cluck
Can't duck
End loose
Cook goose
So long
Swan song

Reign Checks

Realms flow
Kings go
Guile game
Stays same
Crowds cheer
Then jeer
Seek knights
End fight

Pawns shift
Crowns drift
Home rules
Rook fools
Queens play
Odds sway
Last state
Checks mate

Line Tame

Crowds wait
Hug gate
Claw push
Growl shush
Long file
Squeeze pile
Near prey
They stay

Cat like
Set strike
Curse scoff
Till off
Asked please
Mind Ps
Don't stew
Keep queue

Scratch Off

Leash hold
Pets bold
Bark brave
Rant rave
Loud noise
Tough poise
Words say
Sit stay

Some itch
Flee hitch
They ache
Spring break
Turn tail
Hit trail
Next dawn
Dog gone

Pet's Peeves

Pups chew
Dogs true
As grow
Loves show
Barks plead
Their need
Here's how
Hugs wow

Kits play
Cats lay
Groom fur
May purr
They fuss
Ask us
Kow tow
More bow

Bull's Eye

Cows wink
Males blink
Same Shtick
Quick trick
His half
For calf
Good Mood
For dude

Love not
Big shot
Must do
One two
Serve spark
Hits mark
Proves stud
No dud

Cat Calls

Pets hear
Shouts near
First pup
Turns up
Runs quick
Jumps lick
Dogs come
Cats numb

Kits cute
Soon snoot
Snub cues
Choose moves
Won't heed
Your lead
Their sign
Fee line

Cross Words

Clues hid
Patch grid
First try
Just I
Guess work
Seek quirk
Ups downs
Finds frowns

Loose ends
Ask friends
Use books
Check nooks
Get stuck
Curse luck
Swears stress
Speech less

Squares Won

Chess game
Can shame
Those who
Are new
Try crow
They know
Smart way
To play

But when
Face men
Their skill
Proves nil
Moves trounced
Pride bounced
Ends wrecked
Bum checked

Chick Flix

Ads vie
Films try
Bring gals
Their pals
From hatch
Pay scratch
Shows shock
They flock

Best kind
They find
Soap plots
Scenes hot
Some howl
Love fowl
Men group
Fly coop

Gone Pot

Cards dealt
Hopes felt
Eyes flush
Hearts blush
Each draw
Grits jaw
Chips pile
Few smile

Bulls bold
Bears fold
Some joke
Slow poke
Bluff burn
Last turn
Wins now
Cashed cow

Buzz Weirds

Youth joys
New toys
Hot games
Crazed names
Chops chips
Zaps zips
Words chopped
Close cropped

Old squares
Round stares
Mind squirms
Tech terms
Worlds change
Talks strange
More sense
Past tense

Noose Men

Old west
Wild guest
Folks strange
Ride range
Bad? Good?
Knock wood
Tense times
Breed crimes

Fights peeves
Horse thieves
Crooks race
Laws chase
No truce
Hang loose
Old young
High strung

Awe Sum

Buy more
Debts soar
Curbs lax
Cards max
Pain grows
Green woes
Bank bled
Sees red

Bills come
Till numb
Cash flows
Now nos
Craze cools
Heed rules
Stop wrecks
Rein checks

Dust Up

Earth's plan
For man
Play game
Start same
If dud
Stick mud
Then you're
Dirt poor

Those bold
Dig gold
Drill soil
Gush oil
Don't wait
Foil fate
Last ditch
Filth rich

Loan Range

Dear friend
Asks lend
Needs now
Makes vow
Pay back
No flak
Act rash
"Here's cash"

Once grant
Cans can't
Won't pay
Goes way
Past due
Must sue
"Twas steal
Dun deal

Mo Dick

Ish tell
Yarn well
Perq sail
Hunts whale
Seek sight
Rare white
Wild seas
Sweat freeze

Winds rain
Crews strain
End chase
See face
Waves rip
Sink ship
Capt dies
He's prize

Pop's Art

Craft bloom
Dad's room
Paints splash
Slap dash
He's proud
Scenes loud
Works fast
Has blast

Crowds flock
Love shock
Praise jeer
Smirk sneer
Those smug
Shout hug
Rest hear
Deft ear

Broad Ways

Show biz
Froth fizz
Stage struck
Try luck
Brief spark
Then dark
Most flash
Then crash

Rare few
Break through
Frail time
In prime
If hit
Light lit
Fades clout
Lights out

Who Dos

Crime tales
Blood trails
Plot lines
Twists twines
Seek clues
Old news
More bends
Dead ends

Last acts
More facts
Sly look
Name crook
Shots race
Wild chase
Rogue slips
Guilt trips

Bar Flies

Pub scene
They're seen
Hop long
Mix throng
Give hug
Bite bug
Night ends
Part friends

Next meet
Quick greet
Skip dine
Bee line
Where found
Buzz sound
Sting see
Flint flee

Bar Flies2

Pub scene	Next meet
They're seen	Quick greet
Hop long	Skip dine
Mix throng	Bee line
Give hug	Where found
May bug	Buzz round
Night ends	Last see
Part friends	Flit flee

Main Line

Suns perk	End rounds
Dawns work	Home bounds
Eye tears	Day through
Shift gears	Greet crew
Find groove	Back track
Make move	Click clack
Rush down	Toils drained
Big town	Well trained

Squeeze Play

Those wise
Down size
Some crave
Must save
Can't dodge
Hodge podge
Stuffed rooms
Like tombs

Each tier
Most dear
Kin shout
Throw out
No how
Cow tow
Til dead
Bull head

Short Cuts

At work
Some shirk
Smart find
Less grind
On roll
Meat goal
Hot dogs
Leap frogs

Old guard
Stays hard
With butt
In rut
In brief
Just beef
Same place
Cold case

Out Takes

Her wish
Fine dish
Dress up
Out sup
There dine
Fine wine
Top drawer
Gold door

But he
Thought "ME"
His mood
Fast food
Down hill
Went Thrill
End fate
Got gate

Toil Road

Free ways
Cars blaze
Fast lane
Sparks pain
Wives shout
Watch out
She frets
He sweats

His swerves
Test nerves
Her frown
Slow down
End trip
Lose grip
Car tired
Both wired

Hit Run

Some fights
Base rights
Old school
Slugs rule
Where teams
Blow steam
Weak wrong
Smart strong

To last
Swat fast
Words spike
Quick strike
One shot
Quick trot
No err
Foul fair

Nite Lite

New borns
Wake mourns
Their cries
Light skies
Each peep
Kills sleep
Hearts pound
Screams sounds

Mom dad
Both glad
When shrill
Turns still
Queen's nest
Praise rest
Thank lord
Lost chord

Call Girl

Phone crews
Ask views
Claim goal
Take poll
Then heard
Last word
Charge card
Pledge hard

If feel
Won spiel
Push more
Up score
Your choice
Hems voice
When haws
Lost cause

Tag Line

Touch go
Fast slow
Hands flair
Grab air
Each time
That I'm
Near thee
You flee

Love's game
Much same
See blush
Make rush
Ends chase
Wins race
To wit
You're it

Butt Heads

Who's right?
Starts fight
Jut chin
Butt in
First tells
Then yells
Both shout
Butt out

Fool's prides
Take sides
One cool
Names mule
Who walks
Boasts talks
Loves gloat
Gets goat

Heir Cut

Read wills
Tears thrills
Good splits
Score hits
Smiles round
None frown
Those kin
They're in

But some
Feel bums
They boo
May sue
If case
Off base
Laws shout
They're out

I Strain

Her tales
Sad wails
When hear
Shed tear
Drones on
Tho yawn
Each stage
Adds page

Try change
Voice range
To where
Can share
Deaf ear
Won't veer
She spurns
You turns

Imp Pulse

Heart beats
Sweet treats
Love charms
Male arms
Prince sat
Stood pat
His rule
Stay cool

Pot lucks
Pick schmucks
Fool's whim
Crowns him
Sword's voice
Dub's choice
Now rise
"Sir" prise

Miss Fits

Lose things	Times wears
Craze brings	Dulls cares
Once lost	Quests cease
Rooms tossed	Make peace
Search trail	Once quit
Looks fail	Spy it
Words rage	Game through
Blame age	Peek boo

Stale Mates

One wed	Takes two
Each dred	Keep new
Talks drift	Old years
Life Shift	Shift gears
Meals bland	Ease sit
Food canned	Rock knit
Time bare	Mute friends
Oft stare	Dead ends

Air Heads

Tech kid
Gets rid
Old gear
Each year
Must flings
Hot things
Gross size
Net buys

Too soon
Next boon
Makes now
No how
Pen pals
Guys gals
Loves hates
Cell mates

Wise Cracked

Hear quip
Hope hip
Try talk
Lips balk
Mind blanks
Tongue tanks
Pride's plea
Don't flee

So plause
Clench jaws
Brain's fate
Too late
Hope next
Not vexed
Now's stress
Wit less

Cheep Talk

Cell phones
Breed clones
Chicks chat
This that
Quick text
What's next
Costs grand
Out hand

Comes bill
Folks chill
Fowl word
Is heard
Scream shout
Shell out
New regs
Goose eggs

Queue Tip

Check outs
Bring pouts
Lines vast
I'm last
Long wait
Teeth grate
Feet itch
Quick switch

New place
Slow pace
Says voice
Poor choice
"Wear's rule"
Stay cool
Don't Change
Home range

Fire Flies

Eyes greet
Hearts heat
Lights ring
"Real Thing"
Sparks fly
Gal guy
First phase
Hopes blaze

When flame
Turns tame
Flips hot
To not
Thrill ends
Just friends
Cools stress
Match less

Rode Rage

Horse rides
Test prides
When steed
Loves speed
Their pace
Makes race
Clip clop
Won't stop

No whoa
Halts go
His neigh
Wins day
My reins
Aren't reigns
Who's boss?
Sense hoss

Push Pull

Job quests
Take tests
Fill forms
Check norms
Good marks
Spur sparks
If doubt
You're out

Hard work
For jerks
Takes more
To score
Boss choice
Heeds voice
Friends kin
You're in

Reel World

Buy tix
See flix
Screens blaze
Minds glaze
Lights dim
Eyes swim
Crowd sighs
Laughs cries

Time shifts
Weights lift
Stars shine
Blind mine
Their game
Win fame
Our roll
Pay toll

Last Laughs

Sit coms
Oft bomb
When jokes
Need pokes
Fans need
Some lead
Let go
Ho ho

To prime
Fun time
Tapes pour
Canned roar
Techs tout
Their clout
Reel voice
Sound choice

Hold Ups

Folks pledge
Then hedge
Say "but"
Eyes shut
Skip plate
Slow skate
When go
Means no

Time creeps
Then leaps
Debts old
Grow cold
Proud feat
Dead beat
Wills won't
Dos don't

Flash Back

Flames old
Keep Hold
Loves spurn
Still burn
Past fling
Dreams cling
Days daunt
Nights haunt

Friends see
One me
Don't know
Masked woe
That spark
Deep dark
Lurks spy
Mind's I

Come Backs

Grads meet
Hearts beat
Years pass
Spreads class
Old chums
Now 'lums
But cliques
Still clicks

Past thrill
Stays still
Love hang
Same gang
They find
Bonds bind
Stock prize
School ties

Beg Choose

Need cash
Bank dash
Then wait
Check rate
In jam
Act lamb
For now
Kow tow

They swear
All's fare
You brew
Sweat stew
Wait reap
Like sheep
Hope least
Not fleeced

Boo Who

Hide seek
Don't peak
Go slow
Tip toe
Then hear
Laugh near
Friends shout
Jump out

Horse play
Spurs neigh
Clowns gloat
Get goat
Cats scare
Screech stare
Pranks blame
Cry game

Foot Lights

Hearts dance
Gals prance
Shoe fling
Fall spring
Long aisles
Pump styles
Make feet
Walk beat

Spot picks
Get kicks
Sweet fits
Score hits
Hip hop
Non stop
Find great
Sole mate

Guys Things

Bud bunch
Grabs lunch
High slaps
Boots caps
Burge snacks
Sports yaks
Sweet bun
Fast run

Gent's grub
Choose club
Ties coats
Stock quotes
Time slow
Words flow
Ends talk
Cake walk

Match Point

Date game
Odds lame
Choice friends
Dead ends
Dodge blocks
Watch clocks
Seek spot
Best shot

Make pass
Show class
Play sport
Full court
Scratch mark
Find spark
Smoke spikes
Luck strikes

Rump Roast

School daze
Brass haze
Goon squad
Rules quad
Bulls charge
Eyes large
Frosh bow
Kow tow

Some stop
Use chop
Talk glim
Smile rim
Their kind
Smooth grind
Choice bends
Beef ends

Foul Plays

Flix score
Blood gore
Kid's blast
Ghoul cast
Sound blares
Night mares
Thrills spells
Weird sells

Spend cash
See slash
Hot lines
Chill spines
Dark side
Their guide
Ills ails
Gross sales

Stock Yards

Dow cools
Calm rules
Charts flat
Stand pat
Some hold
Shun bold
Saved loot
Bears fruit

Brave charge
Think large
Let flock
Watch clock
Sense highs
Chase buys
More fun
Bull run

Bye Buys

Lived lush
Dreams flush
Felt free
Cards spree
No end
See spend
Till bills
Brought ills

New vow
Start now
Use cash
Stop crash
More home
Less roam
Burst lusts
Boom busts

Clone Prince

Corp lairs
Live squares
All same
Start game
Marks toed
Throne road
Eye prize
Match wise

Each move
Tries prove
Which knight
Moves right
Fit ins
Claim wins
Mate drawn
Crowns pawn

Whose Who

Old age	May shrug
Bumps rage	Blame drug
Names drop	Sluff off
Words stop	Laugh cough
Tongues trip	But fear
Feet slip	Stays near
Free will	Worst plea
Down hill	Who's me

High Bread

Rich oaf	Poor dream
Can loaf	Down stream
Swap boasts	Some bums
Make toasts	Life's crumbs
May work	Work buns
Oft shirk	Neath suns
Stay just	Low reign
Top crust	Food chain

Up Scale

Star slow
Dreams grow
Don't shirk
Hard work
In time
Hopes climb
Sweat tush
Drive push

End race
Where's place?
Still draw
Short straw
Right stuff
Not' nuff
Earn ins
Pull wins

Hang Ups

I phone
Hear clone
Push one
Hopes numb
If told
Please hold
Last look
Give hook

They call
Strange drawl
Cash cries
Ires rise
Try close
Nice nos
Still whine
Dead line

Bed Lamb

Young day
Kids play
Hub bub
Bath tub
Then heed
Sleep need
Games cease
Hug fleece

Turn page
Old age
Talk slow
Nods flow
Bed made
Pull shade
Night knap
Wool wrap

Strut Stuff

Man's pride
Shuns guide
Won't ask
Help task
Cock's walk
Boasts squack
Can't sway
His way

Song fades
Needs aides
Strides slow
Eats crow
Steps stop
Eyes drop
Voice tries
Humm pies

Turn Style

Sales sound
Mobs bound
Hear spiels
Eye deals
Friends urge
Spend splurge
When pelf
Top shelf

Home guilts
Buzz wilts
Now rue
Greed's coup
Once more
To store
Ed tracks
Pay backs

Wits End

Those smart
Talk tart
Quick jokes
Please folks
sharp style
Earns smile
Fans roar
Want more

But if
Crowd stiff
Words rank
Eyes blank
Punch slow
Must go
Last stop
Flip flop

Go Round

Pols dance
Switch stance
Sens reps
Side steps
Pro skill
Say nil
Line plan
Chairman

Once win
Stay in
Hop to
Jump woo
Hands shake
Fast break
Stand greet
Save seat

End Game

Why try
All die
Can't fight
Ump's might
Our stat
One bat
Must go
Life's flow

Hope to
Swing through
Hold ball
Till fall
Can't quit
May hit
Strike shout
"You're Out"

Catch Phrase

Sales pitch
Bait switch
Eyes grab
Hands nab
Try laugh
Get gaff
Ends spin
Reels in

Their wish
Land fish
Earn grin
They win
One bite
Stops fight
Prize look
Right hook

Boon Docks

Who's got
Best yacht?
New rich
Buy pitch
One up
Prize cup
Cruise blog
Top dog

When wish
Go fish
Sail seas
Where please
Boast sports
Pick ports
Win cheers
Show piers

Cause Ways

Hands out	Their prayer
Sobs shout	Beg share
Pleas drone	Sounds dear
Mail phone	Coax cheer
Need great	Matched funds
Don't wait	Raise tons
Words brash	Twice great
Send cash	Checks mate

Cuts Chase

Nice guys	Those tough
Seek prize	Skip bluff
Comes push	Stiff pains
Fall tush	Grab reins
Find game	Blood guts
Not tame	Kick butts
Brute force	One trule
Crash course	Win rule

Stop Watch

Men prime
Mark time
Talk pals
Check gals
May stare
Dream bare
If clicks
Heart ticks

When hot
Feet trot
Swap smiles
Run miles
Turf test
Show best
Right place
Win race

Brass Rings

Spring rite
Dreams bright
Teams race
First place
Sure shot
Wins pot
Ends drought
Pans out

All aim
Stake claim
Make rounds
Grab crowns
Hopes new
Comes through
Not old
Fools gold

Film Flam

New show
Ads flow
Reams typed
Words hyped
Stars tour
Puff purr
Fans wait
Hopes great

First night
Turns fright
Crowds stop
Film flop
Much rave
Can't save
Dad qualms
Buzz bombs

Ride Rage

Love race
Win place
Climb on
Cares gone
High ho
Steeds go
Fun thing
Reigns king

Hit trails
Hills dales
Fox hunts
Tricks stunts
Friends play
Hay day
Joy found
Horse round

Wurst Case

Game day
Teams play
Fans munch
Quick lunch
Can't beat
Taste treat
Down dogs
Like hogs

Twixt buns
Strange ones
Ask not
What's hot
Nor tell
'Neath smell
Think this
'Tis bliss

Fore Casts

Golf Green
Fun Scene
Hit ball
Shout call
Bad guess
Scores mess
Right aim
Ace game

Some say
This play
Mimes Dow
Charts how
Right pitch
Ducks ditch
Good lies
Trap prize

Laughing Stock

Best wits
Soft hits
Pop puns
Spread funs
Come backs
Wise quacks
Show flows
Crowd crows

Key rule
Play fool
Make joke
Self poke
Best charm
Ducks harm
Cheep howl
Called fowl

Pinch Hits

Gals slap
When chap
Gets fresh
Paws flesh
Sparks ire
Screams higher
Quick race
Safe place

Next case
Ball place
Fans roar
Tie score
Right aim
Wins game
Clears dome
Run home

Sheer Fun

Climb high
Mount sky
Steep hills
Test skills
Hearts crave
Boast brave
Grab gear
Face fear

Base camp
Start tramp
Clutch axe
Grasp cracks
Scale cliffs
Snow drifts
Nail hike
Peaks spike

Way Fare

Try trek
On spec
Use bike
Hitch hike
Go cheap
Foot jeep
Sights see
Near free

Round earth
Rome Perth
Worlds crossed
What cost?
Ten C
One G
Price your
"Grand" tour

Slug Feast

Crowds Flock
Love knocks
Sit tight
Cheer fight
Fans flame
Fists game
Stand back
Watch whack

As view
Chomp chew
Steaks high
Gloves fly
Hear pounds
Court rounds
Crunch time
Choice prime

Sports Swear

Game day
Teams play
Fans meet
Life sweet
Two sides
Match prides
All friends
Till ends

Last hour
Things sour
Eyes clench
Words stench
Ires flow
Shout "NO"
Score cursed
Damns burst

Tee Time

For males	While hers
Links trails	Cup pours
Guy stuff	Sit chat
Play rough	This that
Bet green	Game sweet
Par scene	Add treat
Keep score	Both cool
Drink more	Club rule

Home Brood

Some souls	Friends scoff
Dig holes	Take off
Their foot	Born stay
Stays put	Home way
Heart pegs	Less noise
Their legs	More joys
First base	Stick round
Their place	Squares found

Hail Storm

Big game	Runs kicks
Score same	Clock ticks
Each team	Last play
Spouts steam	All pray
Both plea	Pass bold
Bless me	Catch hold
Fans din	World lands
Plead win	His hands

Screen Tests

Night dawns	Minds drown
Set yawns	Dumb down
Days weeks	Pix please
Eye seeks	Stress ease
Laughs crime	Find friends
Prime time	Woes end
Lights dance	Tube sits
Bring trance	Dims wits

Flash Pan

What's name?
Stars fame
First phase
Loud praise
Hype deed
Warp speed
They win
Outs in

When lights
Aren't bright
Head lines
Lose shines
Gold crown
Melts down
Gone shout
Ins out

Pair Rants

Kids bring
Fresh spring
Cute noise
Mixed joys
They are
Bright star
Tho stressed
Twice blessed

Soon scene
Goes teen
Time best
Leave nest
Rows cease
Home peace
Ends numb
Two sum

Gone South

Dix land
Life grand
Loves clash
Red Ash
Prides soar
Comes war
Bloods sins
North wins

Next stage
Folks rage
She'll fret
Weds Bret
Gets rich
Stays bitch
He'll scram
Say damn

Bore War

Tough luck
You're stuck
Staff talk
Can't walk
Try move
Glued groove
Must sit
Teeth grit

Words dull
Numb skull
Eyes bleep
Fight sleep
Squirm seat
Hear beat
Ho hums
Dolt drums

Ads Age

Blogs pop
Non stop
Screens surge
Stars urge
Be quick
Just click
Day long
Sell song

Urge spend
No end
Hope greed
Trumps need
Mind pleas
Cease sprees
What's heard
Buy word

Pay Offs

Man's woes
Cash flows
Loves buy
Live high
Not hard
Use card
Debts joint
Gross point

Must cure
Cease poor
Charge not
Save lot
Best thrills
No bills
Sharke's pain
Nets gain

Food Fast

Time lunch
Crowds bunch
Plan one
Do done
Join lines
Quick dines
Grope cash
Then dash

Shun slow
Grab go
In haste
Brief taste
Meals cram
When scram
Mind churns
Heart burns

Lawn Gone

Fade snows
Green grows
Spring boom
Bud blooms
Sow seeds
Mulch feeds
Once more
Hopes soar

Each year
Fresh spear
Race hard
Best yard
Sun's surf
Toasts turf
Dreams beat
Dead heat

Write Ways

First tries
Seek wise
Need tips
Skip slips
Heed chat
"Do that"
"Try this"
Can't mis

My guide
May chide
Helps think
Dodge clink
Won't dwell
In cell
Prime aim
Pen name

Hides Out

Beach fun
Surf sun
Sand scene
Sculpt seen
Kids splash
Teens dash
Old fade
To shade

Gals cute
Skimp suit
Eyes glued
Near nude
Chicks romp
Guys stomp
Buff acts
Bare facts

Grown Up

Bane's age	Next stage
Blank page	Less rage
Folks can	Old cares
Make plan	Not theirs
Set rules	Can't shove
Pick schools	Just love
Your voice	They'll be
Right choice	Their me

Fume Gate

For puff	Try pills
Times tough	Patch ills
Halt smoke	Cure whiffs
Cease choke	No iffs
Stop hacks	Gone brands
In tracks	No ands
Use fans	Takes guts
More bans	No butts

Bone Heads

World news
Vile views
Same woes
New lows
Vain hope
Most cope
Old cry
Why try

Who rules
Oft fools
Brave fight
Make right
Odds frail
Most fail
'Neath crown
Dumb frown

Shore Points

No brakes
Spring breaks
Tails fins
Sun sins
Youth drools
Troll pools
Hope bronzed
Hook blonds

Sail sea
Splash spree
Surf sounds
Pulse pounds
Guys gog
Hot dog
Seek funs
Beach buns

Glass Act

When dine
Choose wine
First show
You know
Right rite
Red White
Your voice
Best choice

If quests
Sniff tests
Don't blush
Say hush
Hang tough
Boast bluff
Last course
Brut force

Top Not

Young flush
Hair lush
Trim mild
Some wild
Blow dried
Puff pride
Their peak
Male chic

Yet when
Turn men
Then try
Cheat lie
Dyes pants
Comb slants
Last place
Bald face

Show Off

First night	If crowd
Play's plight	Not loud
Cast quest	Scenes cold
Act best	Fools gold
Try outs	Then strain
Seek shouts	In vein
Hope views	Last stand
Good news	Gets panned

Buzz Words

Beach scene	Pests charge
Sun screen	Strings large
Bugs blitz	They clump
Give fits	Wham jump
Use traps	Beg aid
Swift slaps	Stop raid
Try sprays	Plead scream
Horde stays	Swat team

Abs Sense

Sad state	Long haul
Man's weight	Swim crawl
Bad sign	Sweat lift
Waist line	Pounds shift
Stop gain	Last leg
Start pain	Lose keg
Small lunch	Bring back
Big crunch	Six pack

Barn Storm

Pols win	Fat cows
Stay in	Push plows
Work charm	Love pace
Bet farm	Horse race
Sow oats	Burst stall
Reap votes	Win all
Hands pump	Whole hog
Stomp stump	Top dog

Times Out

Life's plan
Brief span
Hours drag
Hopes sag
Days go
Slow mo
Years zoom
Bodes doom

There comes
Aches tums
Dulls ire
Cools fire
Too late
Tocks fate
Clocks tricked
We're ticked

Aged Rock

Song scenes
Fans teens
Noise reigns
Ear pains
Loud hits
Teeth grits
New shakes
Earth quakes

Once when
Cave man
Made tones
Used stones
Their sounds
Broke grounds
All told
Rocks rilled

Game Plans

Work done
Seek fun
Man's wish
Hunt fish
Gun poles
Trecks strolls
Catch ease
Shoot breeze

Great trips
Woods ships
Out doors
Thrill soars
feats tell
Lies swell
More brag
Tales wag

Tick Tox

Face fears
Late years
Skin sags
Eye bags
Vain seek
Save peak
In truth
Keep youth

Try tricks
Looks fix
Pay lots
Tucks shots
Main task
Mould mask
Time blocks
Stop clocks

Oh Zone

Loud pounds
Bring Zounds
Drums blaze
Eyes daze
Songs boom
Aches Zoom
Swap Zest
For rest

Noise Zaps
Cause naps
Needs days
Flee craze
Loose cloze
Help doze
Sweet breeze
Catch Zees

Golds Age

Young praise
Rich ways
Hope clutch
Gold touch
Life glows
King's rows
Chase dreams
Sun beams

When old
Rough road
Wheels spun
None won
Rain bows
End shows
You've got
Just pot

Last Ditch

Dead found
Grave ground
From earth
Leave worth
Kin meet
Heads neat
Sit still
Hear will

Cut off
Curse scoff
Rich praise
Part ways
Each gift
Brings rift
End shares
Split heirs

Hop Scotched

Kid's game
Switch blame
Plead no
Jump go
All's fun
Then run
With luck
Pass buck

You're it
Quick flit
Don't halt
Change fault
Find next
Make vexed
Life scheme
Tag team

All Tolled

Watch clock
Tick tock
Those old
Feel cold
May lurch
Go church
Sins pay
Kneel pray

Who knows
Life's close
Dims spark
Dawns dark
Earth spins
Time wins
Last bell
"even "ell"

Life Lines

Years creep
Plow deep
Crows feet
Walk beat
Eyes bag
Rest sag
Fight back
Mask track

Creams soothe
Sands smooth
Save youth
Hide truth
Age curse
Saps purse
Vein race
Saves face

Off Base

Night out	Oft told
Run about	Find gold
Lights flash	Right pitch
Win cash	Strike rich
Hit slots	Win set
Jack pots	Safe bet
I play	Swing flee
They pay	Home free

House Rules

Each man	Folks lead
Has plan	Kids heed
In brief	Young mind
One chief	Old kind
Home base	Moms guide
Best place	Dads chide
Check stir	Prime phrase
"Yes Sir"	"No ways"

Pin Pals

Old days	New kids
Nice ways	Use grids
Kind thoughts	Swap tales
Were taughts	E Mails
Folks wrote	Now greet
Neat note	By tweet
True friend	Hi's Raves
Stamp send	Air Waves

Dead Lines

When Gone	Old Age
Sad Song	Reads Page
Brief Note	As Friends
Short Quote	Meet Ends
Life Acts	Shed Tear
Cold Facts	Toast Bier
That's It	Such Sights
Says Wit	Last Writes

Run Downs

Men are
Like car
First years
Few fears
Great shapes
Small scrapes
Wheels shine
Life fine

As age
Sore stage
Parts rust
Leak bust
Squeeks sound
Faults found
Slow pace
Crank case

Hard Knocks

Fall downs
Bring frowns
Those slips
Life's blips
Could cry
Or sigh
Mouth shuts
Pain butts

Real men
Know when
Stop whine
Find spine
Stand tall
Each fall
Fight flaps
Bum's raps

Checks Up

Crick cracks	Since aches
Goes back	Aren't fakes
Nails shoot	Pay Doc
To root	Costs hock
Can't be	My pains
Not me	His gains
Stabs feel	Health field
Too real	Well healed

Shrink Age

Young wed	Done fuss
One bed	Just us
Kids grow	Make piled
Goods flow	Less wild
Stuff more	Gone gear
Must store	Things deer
High point	Last owns
Jammed joint	Bear bones

Weak Ends

Wife asks	Jobs mired
Help tasks	Soon tired
So man	So quit
Plots plan	Must sit
Use smarts	Paid dues
Draw charts	Off shoes
Keep scores	Time slacks
For chores	Kick backs

Primed Time

What age	Climb steps
Best stage	Slow peps
First phase	Years leap
Youth days	Pains creep
Clocks crawl	Look round
Days stall	Bells sound
Can't wait	Think young
Next state	Top Wrung

Sound Bites

Song new
Chomp chew
Stars chant
Gnash rant
Lights swirl
Crowds whirl
Oft find
Teeth grind

Old still
Shun shrill
Flee blaze
Seek graze
Wish dine
Fine wine
Leave waste
Choose taste

Dam Age

Curse time
Woes Climb
Cheeks sag
Eyes bag
Fault lines
Sad signs
Tick tox
Strain locks

Curses tried
Stem tide
Skin creams
Hold dreams
When told
Look old
Flood fears
Burst tears

Old Saws

At schools
Learn rules
Past lore
And more
Wise phrases
Earns praises
Smart view
Cuts through

Wit's bite
Chews trite
With age
Grows sage
Yet 'neath
Grit teeth
Sharp heard
Buzz word

Pullets Prize

Barn Yard
Life hard
First acts
Eggs cracked
Coop scene
Flock mean
Those juiced
Rule roost

Hard boil
Peck toil
Their stay
One way
Soon fate
Hot plate
Last cluck
Pots luck

Touch Go

What time	Some how
Proves prime	It's now
Clocks click	Main grief
Years quick	Life brief
Youth's haste	Man mad
Much waste	Soon sad
Sands fast	Last scoff
Rush past	Ticked off

Time Lion

Born wild	None cage
Cute child	King's rage
Learns laws	Roams free
Sharp claws	Weak flee
Pounce prey	Life long
Main stay	Lives strong
Pride reigns	Age tames
Food chains	End games

Bye Laws

Bad rules
Bind fools
Blind trust
A must
Once ink
Don't think
First heard
Last word

Hope brave
Can save
Those wise
Will rise
Stop craze
Mule ways
Reign hence
Horse sense

Poll Ticks

Vote time
Hopes climb
Loud voice
Chimes choice
Tight race
Keep pace
Count hours
Taste powers

Chart trends
Watch friends
Hands spin
Counts in
Last click
First pick!
Room rocks
Cleaned clocks

Pay Daze

Schools teach
Profs preach
Rave rant
Lib slant
Spin scores
Class wars
Grads learn
Left turn

When 'lums
Job numbs
They stare
Tax share
Soon find
Change mind
See light
Turn right

Faux Pause

Vain boast
Brag most
Proud claims
Drop names
Buy fake
Then make
Big tweet
Deals sweet

Friends tell
Sham sell
Their talk
Ends squawk
Was rooked
Goose cooked
Ends show
Eats crow

Real Deal

All in
None win
That's nub
Join club
Have chair
All's fair
Till round
Die mound

Game on
Soon gone
Full deck
Bet check
Best part
Take heart
Get paid
In spade

Just Ice

News sad
Most bad
Check dolts
Nuts bolts
Goats sought
Till caught
Cool hailed
Good nailed

Heats loud
Please crowd
Truth spurned
Pure burned
Cold facts
Lambs axed
Those prude
Get screwed

Sad States

Gov Jobs
Spawn snobs
Perks spoils
Less toils
Lean back
Chat snack
Lines churn
Folks burn

Laws grow
Forms flow
All dread
Tape red
Rules new
Face blue
Gone fight
Flag white

Klutz Hit

Pros talk
Chat squawk
Love sprew
Foul view
Sports plays
Few praise
Fore casts
Oft blasts

Last word
Fans heard
Their cash
Makes smash
These scores
Stun bores
Flip flops
Spin tops

Turn O'er

Polss grin	Polls slip
Hope win	Lose grip
Same feat	Must dote
Save seat	Next vote
Skip scams	Words shift
Film flams	Goals drift
Try stop	Switch pace
Flip flop	'Bout face

Stump Stomp

Vote scene	Must go
Pols preen	Toe toe
Staffs dance	Hold peps
Polls prance	Watch steps
Foot race	Glides win
Fast pace	Shoe in
Brag boast	March gains
Cheer toast	Champ pains

High Ball

March mad
Fans glad
Wait year
Fresh cheer
Long lines
Pump signs
Teams moan
Claw throne

Throngs sweat
Boast bet
Ranks change
New range
Those top
Fear flop
Scores toll
Heads roll

Fan Males

Crowds scream
"Our Team"
"Neath skin
Like kin
Who's best?
Slap chest
When done
We won

Hard core
Cheer more
Dry spells
Won't quells
Can't scorch
Their torch
Those flames
Got games

Fast Track

Each score
Fans roar
Praise those
Old pros
Their steam
Boosts team
Work buns
Raise runs

New guy
Gets try
Wows crowd
Screams loud
Drives swift
Give lift
Hoist Names
Haul fame

Last Stands

Big crowd
Roars loud
Tease scoff
Stand off
Foes curse
You're worse
Refs cry
Stand by

Play rough
Both tough
Praise shout
Stand out
Ends scream
Best team
Wins cup
Stand up

Run Round

Sports jog
Wind fog
Sleet snow
Still go
Long miles
Smug smiles
Change pace
Love race

We praise
Their ways
Just sit
Watch fit
They Strain
In rain
Brag wet
Know sweat

Frame Ups

When bowl
Feel whole
Throw ball
Give all
Fast lanes
Ease pains
Spares strikes
Spike psychs

Watch pros
Smooth throws
Hooks curves
Soothe nerves
Times good
Knock wood
Top score
Bowled 'Ore

Love All

Balls go
To fro
Fast pace
Swift ace
Miss lob
Scow; sob
Blame wind
Noise din

Stars loud
Court crowd
Show dash
Swing smash
Outs lets
Faults sets
Can't catch
Met match

Touch Down

Day done
Home run
Hit ground
Safe sound
Slow chase
Rat race
Rest joints
Sore points

Game plan
Calm man
Yawn stretch
Break catch
Let go
World's woe
Aches mend
Dead end

Ad Vice

Half truths
Tease youths
Read blurb
Claims heard
Please try
Beg buy
Heed shout
Cash out

Hope greed
Sprouts need
Trust ads
Join fads
Close sales
Their grails
No sin
Cash in

Card Sharks

Game day
Pros play
Cards dealt
Thrills felt
Chairs manned
All hands
On deck
Raise check

Chips in
Sly grin
Fives tens
Big bens
They eye
Small fry
Their wish
Shell fish

Shrink Raps

Psych songs
Sing wrongs
First line
I'm fine
Change pitch
Hit switch
Foul ball
Tell all

Stars pose
High lows
Scram sins
Stage spins
Crowds frown
Wind down
Tight beat
Rap sheet

Thumbs Rule

She asks
He tasks
Pound nails
Swing fails
Oops slip
Curse grip
Who's fool?
Blame tool

His vow
Learn how
New look
Buys book
But aim
The same
Next slide
Blame guide

Dis Cuss

Teens shout
Scream flout
Foul words
In herds
From mild
To wild
No pride
Free ride

Low class
Like brass
Pray soon
Change tune
Shocks pale
Turn stale
They scoff
Swear off

Sole Mates

Shoe sale
Like grail
Fads in
Fem's sin
Must try
Then buy
Great styles
Huge piles

No lure
So sure
Makes gals
Life pals
Don't fight
This rite
You'll meet
Dos feet

Lost Cause

Phone pleas
Beg please
New mails
Bring tales
Fill need
With speed
Which one
Or none

We should
Do good
Yet scores
Breed more
So most
Are toast
When pled
For bread

Got Cha

Dance craze
Wins praise
Watch pros
Head toes
Lads lass
Show class
Feet fly
Trip try

Step one
Have fun
Some win
Shoe in
Fear not
Last spot
Joys burst
Feat first

Just So

Bad days
Crime pays
Weird rules
Let fools
Off hook
Shield crook
They flee
Guilt free

Rich too
Sail through
Puff pout
Soon out
Laws err
Hot air
Poor sag
Hold bag

Up Braid

Top news
Big dos
As stars
Go far
Loves change
Looks strange
Find fame
Head game

Their form
Scorns norm
Seek raves
Shock waves
Hot cool
Fans rule
Wild reigns
Hair brains

Block Busts

Brass view
Films new
Give go
Big show
Ads hype
Star type
Then wait
Check gate

Crowds flock
Gold crock
Can boast
Raise toast
Fans shun
Flop done
Boom is
Just fizz

Spot Lite

From blue
Star new
Flash fame
Blaze name
Crowd wowed
Roars loud
Signs high
Lights sky

Sun blinds
Cloud minds
They fear
End near
Sparks flit
Fans split
Fades clout
Lights out

No Nos

Fed's tools
Flood rules
From hills
New bills
Add laws
No pause
Those codes
Tax lodes

Folks roar
No more
Hate regs
Loath negs
Drop dead
Tapes red
Fear aughts
Dread naughts

Self Taunt

Those stressed
Bomb test
Bad days
Walk dazed
Need break
Cure shake
Stop shout
Chill out

Guts tied
Can't hide
Must sit
Cool it
This cold
Morphs old
Makes hots
What knots

Take Charge

Banks shout	When shop
Cash out	Quick stop
Use card	All's fine
Less hard	Just sign
Pay day	Mail run
Far way	Bills stun
Here's how	In hock
Switch now	Shill shock

What Gives

Hear yea	Sales surge
Pledge plea	Beg urge
Drives tout	Share loot
Give out	Give hoot
Mails phone	Stress quilt
Same tone	Till wilt
Push spin	Shove cup
Give in	Give up

Bad Guise

Pix Show	First reel
Soon know	Crooks steal
Black Hats	More gore
Are rats	Crimes score
Old plots	Knight comes
Fight shots	Beats bums
Hit run	Love glam
Still fun	Film flam

Bad Guise2

See show	First reel
Soon know	Crooks steal
Black hats	Comes gore
Are rats	Crimes score
Old plots	Knight comes
Fights shots	Beats bums
Hit run	Love scam
Still fun	Films scam

Hump Dump

Back when	Now told
King's men	Tale old
Held helm	Those tall
Ruled realm	Will fall
Tough yeggs	Trust none
Cracked eggs	Will done
They broke	Fate same
Kept yoke	Shell game

Fast Talk

Comes Lent	Some feel
Time spent	Skip heal
Past deeds	Why tell
Soul's needs	All's well
Life's aims	Won't rest
Faults blame	Take test
Pray pause	Vow naught
God's laws	Food thought

Knock Downs

Style highs	Till then
Rich buys	Find den
Price tag	Not store
Big drag	Clone war
Must haves	Break law
Save halves	Buy faux
Find way	Try skat
Less pay	Cop that

Fire Range

Top guns	Those low
Plot runs	Skip show
Brave quest	Don't try
Prove best	Bulls eye
Good show	Keep job
Gung ho	Stay mob
Sole aim	Blind spots
Win game	Big shots

Cons Test

Checks mail	Words feed
Game tale	Man's greed
Ads glow	Cast bait
Hypes flow	Then wait
Their pitch	Catch look
Get rich	Snare hook
Near free	End Chain
Small fee	Net gain

Dunce Deal

Don't sign	If skip
Dot line	Act flip
Till squint	Then crooks
Fine Print	Own hooks
You must	You're caught
Not trust	Gain naught
Words said	Can't win
Else dead	Dun in

Day Shift

Time change
Sleep strange
Toss rock
Check clock
Teeth grind
Tell mind
Morn noon
Come soon

At farm
no 'larm
Cows skip
Time flip
They ban
Man's plan
Change none
Milk run

Fowl Play

Pols game
Not tame
Poor plead
Chick feed
No bucks
Dead ducks
End dreggs
Goose eggs

Those in
Cluck grin
Cock sure
Their lure
Hatch plots
Vote lots
Rich boost
Rule roost

Wise Guise

When scene	Don't cave
Grows mean	Be brave
Act tough	Look large
Make bluff	Take charge
Strike pose	Eyes cross
Sneer nose	Like boss
Hope foe	Crime Don
Goes slow	Pro con

Ring Sides

Sad sights	When near
Threats fights	Sprouts fear
Shouts loud	Moods change
Mills crowd	Friends strange
Those mild	Strong stay
Turn wild	Plan A
Spikes mean	Weak flee
Mob scene	Plan B

Last Straw

Pols meet
Schmooze greet
Seek votes
Reap dotes
Praise hicks
In sticks
Hope field
Good yield

Grass roots
Are hoots
Brag deeds
Sow seeds
Win day
Make hay
If fail
Must bale

Bull Pen

When write
Use might
Grab horns
Break norms
Think large
Then charge
Tame words
In herds

Cow boys
Use ploys
Spur sweet
Find meat
Weak bland
Strong brand
Steer takes
High steaks

Clap Trap

Teens talk
Scream Squawk
Hot phones
Text tones
Heave huff
Spout fluff
Leave cold
Those old

While they
Prate play
Hands flair
Thin air
Their tweet
Lacks meat
Vain chat
Chew fat

Pen Pals

Men bless
Cave mess
Dawn 'lvn
Hog 'evn
Sty stays
All days
No fuss
Leave muss

Wives mope
Try cope
But neat
Tough feat
His style
Food pile
Gorge shout
Pig out

Sell Phone

Those rings
Oft brings
Gift pleads
Dire needs
Voice drones
Sweet moans
You bluff
Hang tough

Next try
Nice guy
They push
Snub shush
Last call
Stop stall
No yup
Hang up

Stock Picks

Bulls swarm
Bet farm
Hope for
Big score
Check field
For yield
Risk pain
Reap gain

Old crowd
Not cowed
Bum steer
Costs dear
Flawed quotes
Make goats
In brief
Where's beef?

Stock Marks

Young slave
Try save
Cash flow
Must slow
Oft choose
Soon lose
Hot tips
Turn rips

May go
Wrong pro
Who feeds
On greed
Risks bread
Zones red
Burns most
Cold toast

Eye Spy

Watch block
Round clock
My range
Check strange
Gut feel
False real
My goal
Find mole

On square
New pair
Mull why
So shy
Is our
Next door
Stock blond
James bond

Marks Time

Two males	Man poor
Hear tales	Bites lure
Choose stocks	Buys now
Hot rocks	Risks Dow
Pros claim	Chews blogs
Beat game	Grounds hogs
Smart blink	Stops poke
Pause think	Gopher broke

Hands Out

Mail call	So pause
Stacks tall	Check cause
Still see	Best shout
Cash plea	Wins out
Same drift	Gut voice
Need gift	Heart's choice
Which pile	Right rings
Worth while	Palm springs

Gold Horde

Pros pitch
Get rich
Here's how
Beat Dow
Choice picks
Coins bricks
No sweat
Safe bet

Stock pile
Worth wile
This stash
Tops cash
Those bars
Stay stars
Life's key
Gilt free

Street Smarts

Stock swings
Bring strings
Bad news
Leaves bruise
Each bump
Hearts thump
Dow falls
Bang walls

Charts turn
Stakes burn
Learn take
Else break
If strain
Much pain
Says code
Hit road

Cold Calls

Press touts
"Watch out"
Storm near
Feel fear
Winds blow
Big snow
Broad cast
White blast

Comes day
Skies gray
Few flakes
Sun breaks
Wolf's cry
Was lie
News spin
Sheep grin

Hedge Hog

Work slave
Scrimp save
Pick stock
Earn shock
Hot tips
Lose chips
All tries
Down size

Need pros
trim lows
They claim
Sharp game
So try
Their buy
Cuts worse
Trims purse

Top Notch

Bald peeks
At peaks
Must halt
This fault
Good tress
Stops stress
Seek new
High do

Try fit
Close knit
Make crown
Not clown
Let waves
Win raves
Till grooms
Hair loom

Shots Snap

Phone pix
Quick clicks
No fees
Worth sees
Scrap books
Old looks
Less risks
On disks

Good but
Soon glut
Freeze frame
Brief fame
Old wows
Not nows
News span
Flash pan

Fowl Bawl

Gals once
Played dunce
Cooped up
Dawn sup
Try best
Nurse nest
Their tears
Male fears

Fair sex
Hen pecks
Guys faun
Egged on
Duck blame
Cry shame
Need boost
Rule roost

Sham Pain

Babes sigh
Quick dry
Tears spurt
When hurt
Their plea
"Help me"
Mom snugs
Then hugs

Kid's curse
Love nurse
Brave tough
Right stuff
When grown
Stiff moan
Make grade
Man made

Knight Light

First youth
Trusts truth
Comes plight
Flee fight
Darks win
Praise sin
King's might
Wrong rite

Those small
Take fall
Stay pure
Play cure
Sky scan
Brave man
Stands strong
Rights wrongs

Long Runs

Man's race
Has pace
Starts small
Creep crawl
Grows pep
First step
Walk phase
Swift saves

Next tack
Fast track
Stint schools
Work rules
Slow trips
Stair slips
Life's dregs
Last legs

Heal Toe

Kids rip
Then trip
Feet stub
Need rub
Hurt sigh
May cry
Best drug
Mom's hug

When grown
Less moan
More primp
Less limp
Walk proud
Fool crowd
Must hide
Bruised pride

Fit Fits

My size
No prize
Waist grows
Past clothes
Suck in
Friends grin
If squeeze
All tease

Next phase
Change weights
Pride learns
Stem sterns
End gape
Shift shape
Must charge
Buy large

Zip Code

Young age
Teens rage
Curse word
Is heard
Folks rile
They smile
Tempt shout
"Cut out"

Try rule
Keep cool
If chin
They win
Hope tact
Stamps act
Brings pride
Tongue tied

Tong Tied

Guys hang
Form gang
Fun groups
Shoot hoops
Soon find
They bind
Share pride
Choose side

Once in
Thick thin
Tongue true
Like glue
Stick flock
Lips lock
Stay road
Zip code

Sour Suite

Eyes scan
Ship plan
When young
Bells rung
It's price
or nice
Save gold
Stay hold

When lush
Sail plush
Low rooms
Like tombs
With dough
Pipes blow
Top treat
Toots sweet

Friend Ships

First grade
Mates made
Teen time
Pals bind
School too
Guys glue
Grad hits
Groups split

Launch forth
South north
Past crew
Rings true
Last dock
Take stock
When old
Bonds hold

Fool Proof

Thin line
Rough fine
Joke gag
May drag
Hot feet
Cause heat
Back fire
Spark ire

Try scoff
Laugh off
But fate
Too late
Pranks bad
End sad
Brains null
Numb skull

Try Age

Teen snits
Give fits
Wills won't
Dos don't
Moms dads
Bear mads
Pain groans
Fight nos

When ends?
Ask friends
They say
That day
Kids grown
On own
End track
Pay back

Crib Notes

New weds
Mixed dreads
Babes change
Home range
Mom's fears
Switch gears
Can't hide
Dad's pride

Fast scenes
Tots teens
When old
Reach gold
From start
Grows heart
Aches tears
End rears

High Ups

Tell youth
Raw truth
No age
Is sage
Old hat
Stays pat
Likes warm
Keep norm

Young Turks
Gum works
Words hot
Stir Pot
Right heat
Cooks meat
Steaks won
Well done

Age Less

In youth
Tell truth
Pals peers
Know years
Men stay
That way
Gals wait
Change date

Comes grays
Change ways
Less fuss
Years plus
Now loud
Boasts proud
When old
All tolled

Stage Frights

Life starts
Beat hearts
Babes hope
Moms cope
Each year
Face fear
End run
Job done

When grown
On own
Leave nest
Big test
Wheels turn
Pops learn
Now lad
Do dad

Hard Drives

Tots ride
Seats tied
Mom's plan
Take van
Rides long
Chant song
Safe trips
No blips

Years flow
Teens grow
Friend's gift
Give lift
Feel grown
Wish own
Sing stress
Wreck less

Grime Scene

Kid's prize
Mud pies
Their soil
Mom's toil
Splash dirt
Won't hurt
Till stains
Bring pains

Young age
Grunge stage
When boys
Hog toys
Sty scene
May clean
Till then
Pig pen

Gaunt Lets

New birth
Brings mirth
First child
Starts mild
Young years
Joys tears
Next phase
Turns craze

Teen time
Walls climb
Night morn
Stress borne
Goes on
Till gone
Cry glee
Home free

Phase Lift

How young?
Hold tongue
Tell half
Just laugh
No fear
Fudge year
Switch talk
Take walk

Let youth
Blab truth
Wise plan
Fools man
Hide gray
From day
White lie
Do dye

Jump Starts

School done
Ends fun
New grad
Hears Dad
Time flies
Cut ties
Words shout
Move out

Next round
Job found
Now knows
Cash flows
Now chore
Earn more
Gone Pop
Bucks stop

Child Hoods

Play grounds
Sad sounds
Bulls scare
Meek bear
Kids clash
Push crash
Groups mill
Do nil

Smart might
Shun fight
Use wits
Stop hits
Win space
Save face
Duck traps
Beat raps

Kick Backs

Chores done
Earn fun
Gone blues
Off shoes
Home stretch
Fades wretch
This time
My prime

Need place
Slow pace
Calm nerves
Flee curves
Clocks hush
Gone rush
Find sense
Passed tense

View Points

Prof drones
Class moans
They sit
Half wit
Room gray
Thoughts stray
Words dull
Numb skull

Those best
Gush zest
Make cut
Bright strut
Mind thrills
Hone skills
Lose carp
Find sharp

Spring Breaks

Each year
Kids cheer
Leave schools
Skip rules
Love breach
Seek beach
Lives pop
Non stop

Folks cringe
Fear binge
Cats wild
Gone child
Ends tour
Cash poor
Stop ticks
Start checks

Turn 'Bout

In school
Kids cruel
Tots teens
Ways means
Cliques tight
Tout fight
Strong prey
Weak pray

Bide bads
Till grads
Roles switch
Poor rich
Small large
Worms charge
Flip track
Pay back

Mean Life

School place
Minds race
Young ask
Life's task
Profs guess
No yes
Leaves cares
Up air

Grad gates
Swing fates
World hops
Non stops
Stress skips
Falls trips
End jumps
Down dumps

Night Crawls

Tot wails
Sleep fails
Hear cries
Loud sighs
Mates churn
Whose turn?
Short pause
Hems haws

Wed bliss
Means this
Must share
Babe's care
Who'll quell
That yell
Tough call
Hard bawl

Spank Clean

Kids Plea
Not me
Learn game
Shift blame
Bro sis
Boo hiss
Scream fight
Back bite

Folks job
Stop squab
Keep band
In hand
When fails
End tails
Cease yak
Dab smack

Bawl Game

Kids whine
Push line
Squirm hit
Throw fit
Wail howl
Scream foul
Voice shrill
Tests will

Who'll win
Give in
May like
To strike
But swing
Not thing
Yell blame
Cry shame

Hum Bugs

Yule tide
Gifts hide
Stores crowd
Hymns loud
Old songs
Lull throngs
Check list
None missed

'Neath trees
Pile sprees
Comes morn
Gifts torn
Yet stuff
Not 'nuff
Whine same
Bored game

Cry Game

Two teams
Twin dreams
Fans cheer
Goals near
Kick starts
Race hearts
Close game
Shout shame

Score tied
Clock eyed
Key play
Wins day
Ball sails
Crowd wails
Hail call
Long bawl

Learn Ropes

Babe's eyes
Start ties
When tots
Taut nots
One two
Lace shoe
Teen group
In loop

When bored
Cut cord
Pull strings
Do things
Last switch
New hitch
Right twine
Ends line

Air Lines

Once flight
High light
Plane trips
No blips
Hip hop
Non stop
Then class
Turned mass

Now waits
Storm gate
More fees
Seat squeeze
Trudge miles
Clown smiles
Three wing
Wing ding

Mess Age

Moms boom
Clean room
Teens plead
Don't need
No how
Not now
Then shrug
Heap rug

Folks wait
Young's fate
When grown
Have own
Hope bain
Same pain
Kin track
Pay back

Post Grad

School days
Swift haze
Four years
Now blears
Trials tests
Friends feasts
Oft sad
Turned grad

Now look
Scrap book
Each grade
Marks made
Three Rs
Worth scars
Proud fact
Class act

Grouch March

Babes beam
Smile scream
Spout Wails
Have ails
Start soiled
Oft spoiled
Folks hope
Loves cope

Worst rage
Dog's age
Sad schtick
Cuss kick
Make scene
Life mean
Stay pup
Groan up

Stress Test

See Child
Go wild
Mom's shout
Time out
Yell "stop"
Call pop
Such strains
Grown pains

Love colls
Strict rules
Last straw
Grit jaw
Arms poise
Halt noise
Hands flail
Ends tail

Cast Ways

Each fad
Goes bad
What's chic
Fades quick
Clothes yearned
Soon Spurned
Turn trash
Gone cash

But then
New yen
Past rogue
Now vogue
Old style
Worth while
Saved bags
Rich rags

Hem Haw

Skirts go
Yo yo
Gals caw
Rah rah
Guys crow
Ho ho
Dears cry
Buy buy

Styles new
Too too
Her awe
La la
His hah
Ha ha
Bucks fly
Bye bye

Face Facts

Anger speeds
Ups needs
Finds tricks
Will fix
Adds zips
Eyes lips
Must paint
What aint

Blush gloss
Stems loss
Each crux
Saves looks
Stops scoffs
Brush off
None see
Old me

Gold Rush

Dads wait
Too late
Needs gift
Acts swift
His chore
Dash store
First thing
Thinks bling

Now urge
Must splurge
Go fetch
Gold's catch
If fail
Ends tail
In spouse
Dog house

Cool Aide

Wives harp
Look sharp
Stop slouch
Suck pouch
Her plan
Best man
Dress proud
Bland crowd

But pitch
Has glitch
Each please
Brings freeze
He's cold
When told
His shout
Chill out

Iron Age

Seek job
Hob nob
Dress spiff
Pants stiff
Neat shirt
No dirt
Best sell
Look well

To pass
Show class
Top toes
Trim clothes
Pressed suit
Bears fruit
Self sold
Join fold

Head Count

Bells sound
King crowned
Crouds rave
Shock wave
Heir starts
Plays parts
His term
Now perm

Lights blaze
Eyes glaze
Lions roar
Cheers soar
Can't hide
Their pride
Claims clan
Mane man

Step Up

Ball room
Spells doom
My stance
Jinx dance
Feet balk
Just walk
Try hep
Ends schlep

Then learn
Moves turn
How to
One two
Jazz jives
High fives
Judge floored
Ten scored

Down Sighs

Rat packs
Love stacks
Kin shout
"Throw out"
Piles rise
Hide skies
Old bored
Still hoard

Nests mound
High ground
Each inch
Needs winch
Deep dwell
Dark cell
Their grave
Man cave

Halve Knots

Where to?
What do?
First voice
Makes choice
Come crows
Squawk nos
When done
Square one

All pause
Lost cause?
Then naughts
Spar aughts
Half ways
Win praise
Ties group
In loop

Slip Up

Weeks chore
Go store
Smart man
Charts plan
Write needs
Chart deeds
When done
Make run

Cruise aisles
Grab piles
Where's note
I wrote?
Mind blank
Feel rank
Cause stress?
List less

Spend Thrifts

Gal's grail
Find sale
Mark downs
Win crowns
Drop price
Once twice
Bluff scoff
More off

Each deal
Like steal
All means
Save greens
Smart squads
Tight wads
Tags chopped
Bucks stopped

Knicks Knack

Some crave
Buy save
Bric bracs
Form stacks
Each niche
Holds kitch
Hear gnome
Claim home

Yard sales
Rich tales
Pawn shops
Door stops
Proud shelves
Boast elves
In dust
They trust

Chaps Shtick

First boys
Choose toys
When grow
Soon know
More bliss
With miss
Next grad
Soon dad

Man's aim
Pass name
Take chance
Wear pants
There chore
Swim more
Help fuel
Jeans pool

Check Outs

Pix mags
Pulp rags
Wild prose
Shocks pose
No bars
News jars
Flesh flash
Mish mash

Folks shop
Lines stop
Eyes dance
Soon glance
Then spy
Grab buy
Con vulse
Imp pulse

Past Tense

My vow
Do now
Be prompt
Times count
Hopes sag
Feet drag
When done
Last one

Life long
Same song
My yoke
Slow poke
Grave stone
Boasts poem
Here see
Late me

Pill Age

Health wars
Fight sores
Use drugs
Beat bugs
Dose small
Curse all
Docs tout
Knock out

Germs tough
Play rough
May die
Still try
Round two
New crew
Strain win
Next kin

Quick Steps

Born Wean
Tot Teen
School Grad
Wed Dad
Work Rounds
Ups Downs
Wife Bails
Hope Flails

Sweet Fate
New Mate
Wounds Mend
Jobs End
Songs Fade
Dues Paid
Last Beat
Six Feet

Ode Man

Scribes plight
Must write
Mute voice
No choice
Hears call
Scratch scrawl
Can't stop
Lap top

Fast slow
Words flow
Know well
Won't sell
Takes care
May swear
From curse
To verse

Home Spun

He's Pa
She's Ma
Close knit
Tight fit
Life slow
So sew
Their kin
Love spin

Hearts cleave
Words weave
Rough days
Mend ways
Laughs stitched
Stay hitched
Times find
Ties bind

Ahs Me

Keep youth
Whole tooth
Each day
Brush way
If fail
Teeth pale
Or worse
Bite purse

X ray
Shows gray
See doc
Ad hoc
Know drill
Sit still
Costs south
Down mouth

Vice Verse

Some Qoutes
Crib notes
Steal thought
Till caught
Come clean
Just green
Glib talk
Hope walk

Then laws
Close jaws
Pal moan
Cell phone
Friends fink
Bars clink
Now fame
Pen name

Watch Man

Dread sign
Dead line
Eyes blink
Try think
Fear waits
Dire date
Palms sweat
Clocks fret

Some day
Will pay
Cease tricks
Start clicks
End chase
Must face
Ends round
Hands down

Split Heirs

Man dead
Will read
Those dear
Wait hear
Hopes soar
Who'll score
They wait
Sealed fate

Terms flow
Some crow
Smiles frowns
Ups downs
Mid shock
Take stock
Clears smoke
Bonds broke

Line Up

Round pool	Who'll tame
Young drool	Wild game
Fish eyes	All wait
Hunt prize	As bait
Girls set	Play loose
Drop net	She's noose
Smiles looks	Clothes taut
Cast hooks	He's caught

Bid Asked

When pro	Here's deal
Says go	What's real
May try	When twist
Bet buy	Count tricks
Bridge gaps	Your call
Watch traps	Risk all
If con	Not sham
Move on	Grand slam

Shore Things

No brakes
Spring breaks
Tails fins
Sun sins
Youth drools
Troll pools
Hope bronzed
Hook blonds

Sail sea
Splash spree
Surf sounds
Pulse pounds
Guys gog
Hot dog
Seek funs
Beach buns

Sea Salt

Must boast
Love coast
Wave swells
Shore smells
Winds blare
Wash air
Sun sand
Dream land

Morn wish
Catch fish
Can't fail
Set sail
Ship mates
Cut baits
When done
Gobs fun

Wise Cracks

Earth quakes
Land shakes
Sounds deep
Wake sleep
Shocks rise
Cloud skies
Cold chill
Time still

Try smile
Fears pile
Wide eyes
Must hide
Can't halt
World's fault
Think fast
Laugh last

Dust Mights

Ah choo
Bless you
Tree zap
Weeds snap
Bugs spores
Wage wars
Fight flows
Eyes nose

No rest
Churns chest
Sprays pills
Soothe ills
Hopes bring
Next spring
No gnat
Sneeze at

El Non

Words blast
For cast
Trend shows
Big snows
Scares soar
Rush store
Storm cursed
Plan worst

Clouds flow
Then go
Sun bright
Not white
Folks scorn
False warn
Rants mob
Snow job

Fall Guy

Hear spring
Trees sing
Greens rise
Burst skies
Now sun
Has won
Feel earth
Give birth

Times march
Laws parch
Air cools
Red rules
Leaves bold
Turn gold
Catch gleams
Field dreams

Land Hoe

Dawns spring
Hands sing
Now scene
Things green
Gone snow
Seeds flow
Work soil
Takes toil

Sun rain
Soothe pain
When reap
Not cheap
Dig spend
In end
Find you're
Dirt poor

Skin Game

Come springs
Bloom stings
With warm
Gnats form
Swat wars
Fight scores
Who reigns
Food chains

Bug's plan
Mug man
See pink
Bite drink
Men rave
Swing brave
Wins horde
Flies lord

Rise Shine

Comes dawn
Teens yawn
Mom boss
Tries toss
Yet they
Still stay
Kid's gloat
Gets goat

Next act
Less tact
Times up
Pops pup
Now heard
Last word
Hand throw
Get go

Pool Sides

Friends meet
Gush greet
Words spout
Laugh shout
Groups shift
Thoughts drift
Waves go
With flow

Ring bells
Fare wells
Ebbs talk
Slow walk
Good byes
Tear eyes
Last chime
Swell time

Ho Hummms

Dawn blooms
Bee zooms
Hear drones
Greet clones
Work hard
Buzzz yard
When done
Seeks hun

Night sounds
End rounds
Gone stings
Swarm clings
Now rest
Group nest
Sleep teems
Sweet dreams

Land Scrape

Each spring
Same thing
Plans green
Lawn scene
Big rush
Aims lush
Turf wars
Start chores

Next seeds
Sprout weeds
Raw heats
Down beats
Looks bland
Hot sand
Gloats sun
Well done

Look Outs

Sun Wins
Tan skins
Proud pose
Beach clothes
Teens try
Near fry
Bronze bod
Near god

Those fair
Take care
High heat
Broils beet
Best park
In dark
Red face
Bask case

Green Aches

Grass land
Starts grand
Sow seeds
Hopes breed
But lawn
Turns tawn
Weeds win
Then grin

Seek aid
Pros paid
Grow pains
Pray rains
Work hard
Yet yard
Turf aint
So paint

Act Up

Start young
Bug stung
Child's play
Funs stay
Stage near
Shake spear
Get hooked
Fate cooked

Fame feeds
Parts leads
Broad casts
Thrills lasts
Friends urge
Star surge
Grand slam
Eggs ham

One Ups

What is
Show biz
Old times
Clowns mimes
Stage plays
Broad ways
Films hot
Top spot

Techs change
New range
Tubes fads
Phones pads
All fight
Spot light
Win rage
Up stage

Wait Watch

Heed praise
New ways
Short cuts
Firm butts
Trim thick
Thin quick
Good byes
Old thighs

Each fad
Proves sad
My toils
Just foils
Mocks scale
"You fail"
'Nre be
Fat free

Kick Offs

These days
Dance craze
Fast pros
Flash toes
Stars fight
Spot light
Now hep
Watch step

Brave hearts
Risk starts
Hope kicks
Are picks
Trip once
Feel dunce
Dreams meet
Do feet

Miss Cast

Stars rage
Fight age
Cling youth
Scorn truth
Puff lips
Squeeze hips
Their goal
Young role

Times change
Shift range
From hits
To bits
Gone vamp
Now camp
Script signs
Laugh lines

Flash Mod

Friends text
What next
Names streets
Group meets
May sing
Dance thing
Fun flock
Love Shock

Some go
For show
Till cops
Make stops
Gone hees
Now pleas
End haws
By laws

Play Time

Foot lights
Gild nights
Crowds seat
Wait treat
Casts beg
Break leg
Darks flow
Start show

Hearts flee
Cares free
Each cue
World new
Watch stage
Don't age
There see
Reel me

Song Dance

Show time
Votes prime
Both sides
Waltz strides
Words flow
Tip toe
Tap treats
Down beats

Pros hep
Quick step
Pols spin
Hope win
Get kicks
Drum sticks
Sweet talk
Cake walk

Feat First

Dance fear	Hopes urge
Starts here	Kicks surge
First step	Dodge trips
Shoes schlep	Flaunt hips
Knees balk	Strong yen
Just walk	Scores ten
Want quit	Should win
Must sit	Shoe in

Tap Dunce

Hey feet	No wins
Look sweet	Klutz spins
Be deft	Sad moves
Not left	Miss grooves
Flair arms	Steps slip
Tout charms	Shoes trip
Make mate	No cup
Look great	Jigs up

Stand Up

End day
Tubes play
Old news
Fresh views
Watch clowns
Soothes frowns
Jokes hurled
Laughs world

Wags rule
Poke fool
Price fame
Fair game
Wits sting
Zap zing
Joust done
Jest fun

Last Rights

Good news
God's views
Love wins
Sinks sins
Cools hots
Flesh pots
Praise songs
Drown wrongs

Act two
Thrills through
When youth
Finds truth
Now earth
Shows worth
Low cries
High rise

Blog Jam

Strange scenes
Plague screens
Fools dance
Pets prance
Weird rubes
Flood tubes
Their plea
Watch me

Eyes hook
Laugh look
Brief views
Short fuse
Quick con
Fast gone
Gross game
Net fame

Sounds Great

Songs bring
Own zing
Feel noise
Hear joys
Feet prance
Hearts dance
Rock jive
Feel alive

Each age
Spawns rage
Fans rave
Arms wave
Lips sinc
Eyes blink
Up sweet
Down beat

Hop Hip

Young blaze
Dance craze
Fling arms
Flout charms
Whirl shout
All out
Claim time
Their prime

Old shy
May try
Shake buns
All thumbs
Prove step
Not hep
Ends hup
Jigs up

Spaced Out

Tap keys
Don't freeze
Quick rate
Lines straight
From A
All way
Reach z
Err free

Check work
Eyes jerk
Oh no
Type O
With ease
Mind Ps
Pick choose
Heed Qs

Band Stands

Each age
Owns stage
Their songs
Thrilled throngs
Words prime
Most rhyme
Tunes bright
Lime light

Next phase
New praise
Now joys
Its noise
They greet
Toots sweet
Old plums
Ho hums

Foot Loose

Ball room
Spells doom
Fear choose
Dance shoes
Each step
Looks schlep
All moves
Miss groves

I plea
Not me
My pace
Straight lace
Both feet
Off beat
Slip slide
Tongues tied

Smear Case

Kids play
Paint spray
Street signs
Train lines
Bridge frames
Foul names
Splash site
Dubbed blights

Then bads
Turn fads
Those pows
Now wows
What's dumb
To some
Makes smart
Pop art

Whirl Gig

World spins
Top sins
Wild throngs
Cry wrongs
Hopes rage
Change age
Strong quiz
What is

Pols best
This test
Love tricks
Claim fix
Sweet sounds
Make rounds
Game on
Pro con

Pop Tops

Casts ache
Big breaks
Find fame
Make name
Light flash
Acts smash
Crowds crush
Life lush

High peak
Fear leak
Coke ales
Fizz fails
Must move
Keep groove
Stand pat
Fall flat

Choice Words

Tales told
Best bold
Fact based
Lacks taste
For wins
Seek sins
Add bite
Then write

In end
Scribes bend
Truth bores
Hot scores
Shake vice
Spritz spice
Right fault
Worth salt

Kiss Met

Does fate
Choose mate
First glance
Big chance
Time stops
Fire pops
One shot
Jack pot

Friends shove
Preach love
Odds slim
Dreams grim
Risk high
When try
She'll scoff
Kiss off

Bush Whack

Pro ball
Starts small
In sticks
Learn tricks
Try leap
From heap
Field pitch
Strike rich

Charge outs
Thrill scouts
Kick butts
Make cuts
Prove goods
Leave woods
Blitz Krieg
Big league

Golfs Coarse

Fine scene	Rough time
Game green	Curse climb
Fun play	Last hole
Fair way	Reach goal
Start game	Once there
Mood tame	Fore swear
Walk hills	Score foiled
Heat ills	Par boiled

Swing Shift

Golf course	Ends match
Fun source	Heads scratch
Spot ball	Drinks jokes
Fore call	Count strokes
Sweet chip	Truth spins
Worth trip	Who wins?
Good putt	Best lies
Earns strut	Scores prize

Old Haunts

Bar clans
Pro fans
Eyes beam
Toast team
Raise beers
Room cheers
Play starts
Boom hearts

Plays foul
Swear scowl
When done
Scream "one"
If two
Hiss boo
Three worst
Claim cursed

Wild Card

Life's real
Raw deal
Each day
Act play
Eye scans
Plot plans
Slow quick
Count trick

Bluffs twists
Clench fists
Good hand
Turns bland
Last call
Bet all
Man bumps
God trumps

Pay Dirt

Fan mags
Oft rags
Snap pix
Sly tricks
They pry
You buy
New tells
Sin sells

Neath earth
Much worth
Rake muck
Gold struck
Flesh pots
Were hot
World's ways
Grime pays

Dough Boys

Cool guys
Toss his
Then let
Caps set
Sit loaf
Look oaf
Stay bums
Earn crumbs

Gents doff
Hats off
Shun couch
Don't slouch
Old schools
Have rules
Rise head
Well bread

Crass Test

Those rude
Act shrewd
Drink quile
Paste smile
Hope grin
Will win
Let pass
Their sass

Works once
For dunce
But twice
Pays price
Booze slurs
Ire stirs
Slam dunk
Punch drunk

Non Plus

Math whiz
Ace quiz
They dig
Calc trig
Know how
Score wow
Minds quick
Fast click

My skill
Proves nil
Not blessed
Like rest
Test books
Blank looks
Tongue tied
Pl eyed

www.ingramcontent.com/pod-product-compliance
Lightning Source LLC
Chambersburg PA
CBHW070639050426
42451CB00008B/223